KIDS ONLY JOKES

Einstein Brothers

BLUE
BIKE
BOOKS

The Publisher: Blue Bike Books
Website: www.bluebikebooks.com

Library and Archives Canada Cataloguing in Publication

Einstein, James Allan, 1977–, author
          Kids only jokes / James Allan Einstein.

ISBN 978-1-926700-48-9 (pbk.)

          1. Canadian wit and humor (English). 2. Wit and humor, Juvenile. I. Title.

PN6178.C3E335 2014   jC818'.602   C2013-906421-4

Project Director: "Mama" Nicholle Carrière Einstein
Project Editors: "Sista" Sheila Cooke Einstein
Author: James Allan Einstein
Cover Images: Front cover illustration: Roger Garcia Einstein; back cover - reindeer © HitToon.com / Shutterstock
Cover Design: Gerry Dotto Einstein
Illustrations: Roger Garcia Einstein, Peter Tyler Einstein
Layout: "Sista" Alesha Braitenbach-Cartledge Einstein

Produced with the assistance of the
Government of Alberta, Alberta Media Fund

$\mathcal{Alberta}$
Government

We acknowledge the financial support of the
Government of Canada through the Canada Book Fund (CBF) for our publishing activities.

Canadian   Patrimoine
Heritage   canadien

PC: 24

Contents

Introduction

This book is for no one but you kids. Don't let anyone read this! Not even your older brother, and especially not your parents. This book contains jokes and funny lines that only kids can understand. If your mother were to pick this up, her face would go all crooked and she would begin to scratch her head. I have written the jokes in a style that only kids may read. It is a known fact (to kids only) that once someone reaches the age of around 15 (for some—mostly girls—it is even earlier) they no longer see the world like a kid. Ask any 15-year-old boy what he dreams about and you might need to block your ears, but ask a kid, and he see the world through an imagination so vast that it is impossible for the older brain to comprehend. There is something in the human brain that shuts down when you hit a certain age, leaving you with no memory of how the world looked when you were a child. Science has never tried to figure it out because scientists are always too old, and they never remember what the world once looked like. I too fell into the adult slumber and forgot about the world I used to see until I came across an ancient book that spoke of the imagination of children. After some further investigation, I used this knowledge and was able to put together a book of jokes that will spark the imagination of kids.

Regaining this view of the world was not an easy task, however. It took me years of practice, meaning, I had to play a lot. Countless hours of sitting in front of the TV watching cartoons and eating junk, whole summers spent outside running through the forest and imagining myself as an ancient warrior sent to slay a dragon, every day doing something that I felt like not because I had to but because I wanted to. I eventually regained the magical powers of childhood and have put them to use to craft this book. I am speaking only to the kids of the world now. Open this book, share the jokes with your friends, and laugh like never before. Sure, you can try telling your parents a joke or two, but they won't understand. Parents never do.

Chapter 1

At School

Q: Why was Rita carrying a ladder?
A: Because she was going to high school.

Q: Why did John walk backward to school?
A: Because it was back to school day.

Q: On what kind of ships do students study?
A: Scholarships.

Prize Money

In tough times, a school offered $50 for the best money-saving idea submitted by its students.

First prize went to the student who suggested the award be cut to $25.

Teacher, Teacher!

Q: Why was the principal worried about his job?
A: Because there were too many rulers in school.

Q: What's the difference between a teacher and a train?
A: The teacher tells you to spit out your gum, and the train says "chew chew chew."

Q: What is a math teacher's favorite dessert?
A: Pi.

Parent-Teacher Interview

Mom: How's my son doing in your class?
Teacher: He surprises me at least once a month.
Mom: In what way?
Teacher: About once a month, he can answer me correctly.

Q: Why did the teacher wear sunglasses?
A: Because his class was so bright.

Q: Why did the teacher turn the lights on?
A: Because her class was so dim.

Q: Why were the teacher's eyes crossed?
A: Because she couldn't control her pupils.

Q: Why did closing her eyes remind the teacher of her classroom?
A: Because there were no pupils to be seen.

Q: What do you do if a teacher rolls her eyes at you?
A: Pick them up and roll them back.

Lies

Two boys are arguing when the teacher enters the room. The teacher says, "Why are you arguing?"

One boy answers, "We found a ten-dollar bill and decided to give it to whoever tells the biggest lie."

"You should be ashamed of yourselves," said the teacher. "When I was your age, I didn't even know what a lie was."

The boys gave the ten dollars to the teacher.

Q: Why did the teacher go to the beach?
A: To test the water.

Q: Why did the teacher write on the window?
A: Because she wanted the lesson to be very clear.

Q: What did the ghost teacher say to the class?
A: "Look at the board, and I will go through it again."

Even Teachers Have Something to Learn

Sandy began a job as an elementary school teacher, and she was eager to help her students. One day during recess, she noticed a girl standing by herself on one end of a playing field while the rest of the kids enjoyed a game of soccer at the other. Sandy approached and asked if the girl was all right.

The girl said she was.

A little while later, however, Sandy noticed the girl was in the same spot, still by herself. Approaching again, Sandy offered, "Would you like me to be your friend?"

The girl hesitated, then said, "Okay," looking at the woman suspiciously.

Feeling she was making progress, Sandy then asked, "Why are you standing here all alone?"

"Because," the little girl said with great exasperation, "I'm the goalie!"

Smart-aleck Students

Student (on phone): My son has a bad cold and won't be able to come to school today.
School secretary: Who is this?
Student: This is my father speaking.

Father: I hear you skipped school to play football.
Son: No I didn't, and I have the fish to prove it!

Teacher: You missed school yesterday, didn't you?
Student: Not really.

careful

A guy is walking past the high, solid wooden fence surrounding the local boarding school for teenage delinquents, and he hears a group of boys inside chanting, "Thirteen! Thirteen! Thirteen!"

He continues walking along the long fence, but, being a curious person, he can't help but wonder why they are chanting "thirteen" over and over. Could it be that they are chugging beer? Are they perhaps taking turns beating one of the younger kids? Maybe they are counting the number of students who been pantsed.

His curiosity peaks, and he searches for a hole in the fence so that he might see what is going on. Finally, he spots one a few feet ahead. The hole is low in the fence, and he has to kneel down to peer inside.

He moves into position and peeks into the hole. As he looks in, someone inside pokes him in the eye! Then he hears everyone inside the school fence start chanting, "Fourteen! Fourteen! Fourteen!"

Teacher: I hope I didn't see you looking at John's exam.
Student: I hope you didn't either.

Teacher: Didn't you hear me call you?
Student: Yes, but you said not to answer back.

Teacher: Didn't I tell you to stand at the end of the line?
Student: I tried, but there was someone already there!

Meeting Plato

In a classroom, pupils were asked to always work in silence. One day, the teacher dozed off and was awakened by some of the pupils making noise. To cover her embarrassment she said, "It was always my wish to meet the scholar Plato, and just now, I did see him in my dream."

The next day, a pupil dozed off while listening to the teacher's long lecture. Upon seeing the sleeping child, the teacher woke him up and rebuked him. "Why are you sleeping during the lecture?"

The pupil answered, "I also went to see the scholar Plato."

The teacher asked, "And what did Plato say?"

The pupil replied, "Plato said he did not meet with you yesterday."

Student: May I go to the bathroom?
Teacher: Only if you can say the alphabet.
Student: Okay. ABCDEFGHIJKLMNOQRSTUVWXYZ.
Teacher: Where's the P?
Student: Halfway down my leg.

Teacher: This is the third time I've had to tell you off this week. What have you got to say for yourself?
Student: Thank goodness it's Friday!

Father: I'm worried about you always being at the bottom of the class.
Son: Don't worry, Dad. They still very much teach the same thing at both ends.

Come Rain or Shine

One morning at the breakfast table, a girl is looking quite cheerful. Her mother asks why.

"Our teacher said we had a test today, rain or shine," the girl told her mother.

Confused, the mother responded, "But I didn't see you studying last night; are you sure you're ready for it?"

"Nope. I was counting on the weatherman being right, and he was. It's snowing!"

Picture Day

The children had all been photographed, and the teacher was trying to persuade them each to buy a copy of the group picture. "Just think how nice it will be to look at it when you are all grown up and say, 'There's Jennifer; she's a lawyer,' or 'That's Michael, he's a doctor.'"

A small voice from the back of the room rang out, "And there's the teacher; she's still old and wrinkled."

Teacher: You're new here, aren't you? What's your name?

Student: Fred Mickey Smith.

Teacher: I'll call you Fred Smith then.

Student: That's no good; my father doesn't like anyone taking the Mickey out of my name.

Q: What's easy to get into, but hard to get out of?

A: Trouble.

Math Problems

Q: What did one math book say to another math book?

A: "Boy do I have problems."

Q: What did the plant do in math class?

A: It grew square roots.

Q: Why shouldn't you do math homework in the jungle?

A: Because if you add 4 + 4 you get ATE!

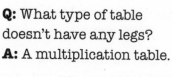

Q: What type of table doesn't have any legs?

A: A multiplication table.

Q: What tables don't you have to learn?
A: Dining room tables.

Q: What did the zero say to the eight?
A: "I like your belt!"

Q: If two's company and three's a crowd, what are four and five?
A: Nine.

Q: Why is 6 afraid of 7?
A: Because 7 8 9!

Q: Why didn't the two 4s want lunch?
A: Because they already 8.

Catholic School

A father who is very much concerned about his son's bad grades in math decides to transfer him to a Catholic school. After the boy's first term there, he brings home his report card—he's getting A's in math. His father is, of course, pleased, but he wants to know why his son's math grades are suddenly so good.

"Well," the boy explains, "when I walked into the classroom the first day and saw that guy nailed to a plus sign on the wall, I knew one thing: this place means business!"

Son: My math teacher is crazy.
Mother: Why?
Son: Yesterday she told us that 5 is 4 + 1; today she is telling us that 5 is 3 + 2.

Classroom assignment: 2 + 2 = 4.
Homework: 2 + 4 + 2 = 8.
Exam: Matthew has four apples, and his train is seven minutes early; calculate the sun's mass.

Teacher: Answer my question at once: what is 7 + 2?
Student: At once.

Teacher: If I had six oranges in one hand and seven apples in the other, what would I have?
Student: Big hands.

Teacher: If five people each give you $20, what do you get?
Student: A new bike.

Teacher: What's 2 + 2?
Student: 4.
Teacher: That's good.
Student: Good? That's perfect!

Teacher: If 1 + 1 = 2 and 2 + 2 = 4, what is 4 + 4?
Student: That's not fair! You answer the easy ones and leave us with the hard one.

Teacher: What is half of 8?
Student: Up and down or across?
Teacher: What do you mean?
Student: Well, up and down makes 3, and across makes 0.

Science and Geography

Atom 1: I just lost an electron.
Atom 2: Are you sure?
Atom 1: I'm positive.

Q: Why can you never trust atoms?
A: Because they make up everything.

Teacher: How is dew formed?
Student: The sun shines down on the leaves and makes them perspire.

Teacher: What is the axis of the earth?
Student: The axis of the earth is an imaginary line that passes from one pole to the other, and on which the earth revolves.
Teacher: Very good. Now, could you hang clothes on that line?
Student: Yes, sir.
Teacher: Indeed, and what sort of clothes?
Student: Imaginary clothes.

A Lesson

A teacher was giving a lesson on the circulation of the blood. Trying to make the matter clearer, he said: "Now, students, if I stood on my head, the blood, as you know, would run into it, and I would turn red in the face."

"Yes, sir," the class said.

"Then why is it that while I am standing upright in the ordinary position, the blood doesn't run into my feet?"

One kid said, "It's because your feet aren't empty."

Q: What is the fibula?
A: A small lie.

Teacher: What does the word "benign" mean?
Student: Benign is what you will be after you be eight.

Teacher: What family does the octopus belong to?
Student: Nobody I know.

Teacher: Can you name two animals that live in a cold region?
Student: A polar bear and his wife.

Son: My teacher was mad at me because I didn't know where the Rockies were.
Mother: Well next time, remember where you put things!

Lunch Meeting

The teacher of the earth science class was lecturing on map reading. After explaining about latitude, longitude, degrees and minutes, the teacher said, "Suppose I asked you to meet me for lunch at 23 degrees, four minutes North latitude and 45 degrees, 15 minutes East longitude?"

After a confused silence, a voice volunteered, "I guess you'd be eating alone."

 I wonder if Earth makes fun of other planets for having no life.

Q: Why is the Mississippi such an unusual river?
A: Because it has four eyes and can't see.

Q: Why is England the wettest country?
A: Because the queen has reigned there for years.

Teacher: Where is the English Channel?
Student: I don't know, my TV doesn't pick it up.

Teacher: What can you tell me about the Dead Sea?
Student: I didn't even know it was sick!

Q: What's purple and 5000 miles long?
A: The grape wall of China.

Know Your History

Q: What is the fruitiest subject at school?
A: History, because it's full of dates.

Mother: Why aren't you doing well in history?
Son: Because the teacher keeps on asking about things that happened before I was born!

Son: I wish I had been born 1000 years ago.
Father: Why do you say that?
Son: Just think of all the history I wouldn't have to learn.

Q: What did Mason say to Dixon?
A: "We've got to draw the line somewhere."

Teacher: What did they do at the Boston Tea Party?
Student: I don't know, I wasn't invited.

Q: Where was the Declaration of Independence signed?
A: At the bottom.

Q: Where does the ghost of Sitting Bull live?
A: In a creepy teepee.

Q: Why does the Statue of Liberty stand in New York Harbor?
A: Because it can't sit down!

Teacher: Abraham Lincoln had a very hard childhood. He had to walk eight miles to school every day.
Student: Well, he should have gotten up earlier and caught the school bus like everyone else.

Teacher: Who gave the Liberty Bell to Philadelphia?
Student: It must have been a duck family.
Teacher: A duck family?
Student: Didn't you say there was a quack in it?

Q: Why did the pioneers cross the country in covered wagons?
A: Because they didn't want to wait 40 years for a train.

Amusing Ancient History

Q: Why were the early days of history called the dark ages?
A: Because there were so many knights.

Q: Who made King Arthur's round table?
A: Sir Cumference.

Q: What was Camelot?
A: A place where people parked their camels.

Q: When a knight was killed in battle, what sign did they put on his grave?
A: Rust in peace.

Q: Where did knights learn to kill dragons?
A: At knight school.

Q: Why do dragons sleep during the day?
A: So they can fight knights.

Q: Where did the king keep his armies?
A: In his sleevies.

Q: How did the Vikings send secret messages?
A: By Norse code.

Q: What do Alexander the Great and Kermit the Frog have in common?
A: They have the same middle name.

Q: What did Caesar say to Cleopatra?
A: "Toga-ether we can rule the world!"

Q: How was the Roman Empire cut in half?
A: With a pair of Caesars.

1st Roman soldier: What is the time?
2nd Roman soldier: XX past VII!

Teacher: When was Rome built?
Student: At night.
Teacher: Why do you say that?
Student: Because my dad always says that Rome wasn't built in a day.

Language Arts Laughs

Q: Why can't S and H ever have a good conversation?
A: Because everyone says "shhh" when they see them together.

Mother: What did you learn in school today?
Son: How to write.
Mother: What did you write?
Son: I don't know, they haven't taught us how to read yet.

Q: What is a witch's favorite subject in school?
A: Spelling.

Q: How is an English teacher like a judge?
A: They both give out sentences.

Burn!

A 50-something teacher asked her students, "If I say, 'I am beautiful,' which tense is that?"

One student replied, "It is obviously past."

Knock knock.
Who's there?
Spell.
Spell who?
W-H-O.

Homework Hilarity

Student: Should I get in trouble for something I didn't do?
Teacher: No.
Student: Good, because I didn't do my homework.

Ideal excuses for not doing your homework:

- I loaned it to a friend, but he suddenly moved away.
- Our furnace stopped working, and we had to burn it to keep ourselves from freezing.
- I lost it fighting this kid who said you weren't the best teacher in the school.
- I didn't do it because then I would have had to hand it in, and I didn't want to add to your already heavy workload.
- I put it in a safe, but lost the combination.

Q: Why did the students eat their homework?
A: Because their teacher told them it was a piece of cake.

Homework Schedule

Here is an explanation of the school homework policy for the average student. As per national guidelines, students should not spend more than 90 minutes per night on homework. This time should be budgeted in the following manner if the student desires to achieve moderate to good grades in his/her classes:

- 15 minutes looking for the assignment
- 11 minutes calling a friend for the assignment
- 23 minutes explaining why the teacher is mean and just does not like children
- 8 minutes in the bathroom
- 10 minutes getting a snack
- 7 minutes checking the *TV Guide*
- 6 minutes telling parents that the teacher never explained the assignment
- 10 minutes sitting at the kitchen table waiting for Mom or Dad to complete the assignment.

Chapter 2

The Animal World

Dogs and Cats

Q: What dog can jump higher than a building?
A: Any dog—buildings can't jump.

Q: Where do you find a one-legged dog?
A: Where you left it.

Q: What do you call a dog with no legs?
A: It doesn't matter what you call him, he still won't come.

Q: Why aren't dogs good dancers?
A: Because they have two left feet.

Q: What did the dog say when he sat on sandpaper?
A: "Ruff!"

Funny Dog

Tim and his dog, Buddy, went to a friend's house to watch a movie. In the middle of the show, Buddy started laughing so hard that he fell off the couch.

"Wow," said Tim's friend, "I've never seen a dog laugh before. That's awesome."

"It sure is," said Tim. "Especially since he hated the book."

Q: What does a lazy dog chase?
A: Parked cars.

Q: Why does a blond dog have lumps on his head?
A: From chasing parked cars.

Q: What do you give a dog with a fever?
A: Mustard; it's the best thing for a hot dog.

Q: What kind of meat do you give a stupid dog?
A: Chump chops.

Q: How do you stop a dog from smelling?
A: Put a peg on its nose.

Q: Why is it called a "litter" of puppies?
A: Because they mess up the whole house.

Q: What do you get if cross two young dogs with a pair of headphones?
A: Hush puppies.

Q: What do you call a litter of young dogs who have come in from the snow?
A: Slush puppies.

Q: Why don't blind people like to sky dive?
A: Because it scares their guide dog!

Q: Why did the snowman name his dog Frost?
A: Because Frost bites.

Q: What is the best time to take a Rottweiler for a walk?
A: Any time he wants to.

Q: What kind of dog chases anything red?
A: A bull dog.

Q: When is a black dog not a black dog?
A: When it's a greyhound.

Q: When does a dog go "moo"?
A: When it's learning a new language.

Q: What do you call a German shepherd in jeans and a sweater?
A: A plain-clothes police dog.

Q: How do you feel if you cross a sheepdog with a canteloupe?
A: Melon-collie.

 In the winter, a dog wears his coat. In the summer, he wears his coat and pants.

Q: What dog loves to take bubble baths?
A: A shampoodle.

Q: Why did the dachshund bite the woman's ankle?
A: Because he couldn't reach any higher.

Q: What do you call a nutty dog in Australia?
A: A dingo-ling.

Q: What do you get when you cross a cocker spaniel, a poodle and a ghost?
A: A cocker-poodle-boo.

Q: What's the dog's least favorite doggy bag?
A: A fleabag.

Q: Why type of markets do dogs avoid?
A: Flea markets.

Q: What did one flea say to the other?
A: "Should we walk or take a dog?"

Q: How do you know that it's raining cats and dogs?
A: When you almost step in a poodle.

Q: What's worse than it raining cats and dogs?
A: Hailing taxi cabs.

- It's raining cats and dogs!
- That's okay, as long as it doesn't reindeer.

Q: What is a cat's favorite color?
A: Purrple.

Q: What does a cat call a bowl of mice?
A: A purrfect meal.

Q: What type of cat purrs more than any other?
A: A Purrsian.

Q: What did the cat do when he swallowed some cheese?
A: He waited by the mouse hole with baited breath.

Q: How do you spell mousetrap in just three letters?
A: C-A-T

Q: What is a cat's favorite song?
A: "Three Blind Mice."

Q: When is it very bad luck to see a black cat?
A: When you're a mouse.

Animal Afterlife

A cat and a mouse died on the same day and went up to heaven. After a couple of days, the mouse met God. God asked, "How do you like it so far?"

The mouse replied, "It's great, but can I get a pair of roller skates?"

God said, "Sure," and he gave him a pair of roller skates.

The next day God saw the cat and asked him, "How do you like it up here so far?"

The cat replied, "It's great! I didn't know you had meals on wheels up here!"

Q: Where did the school kittens go for their field trip?
A: To the mew-seum.

Q: What do you get when you cross a cat with a ball of yarn?
A: Mittens.

Q: What was the alley cat's favorite sport?
A: Bowling.

Q: How is a cat lying down like a coin?
A: Because he has his head on one side and his tail on the other.

Q: What happened when the cat swallowed a coin?
A: There was some money in the kitty.

Q: What is another way to describe a cat?
A: A heat-seeking missile.

Q: Why are cats longer in the evening than they are in the morning?
A: Because they're let out in the evening and taken in in the morning.

on the farm

Q: What do you get from a pampered cow?
A: Spoiled milk.

Q: What kind of things does a farmer talk about when he is milking cows?
A: Udder nonsense.

Q: What did the farmer call the cow that had no milk?
A: An udder failure.

Q: What do you get when you cross a cow with a Smurf?
A: Blue cheese.

Moo Mind Meld

Two cows are hanging out in a field, munching on grass. One says, "Moo."

The other cow says, "Wow, that's so weird; I was just going to say that."

Knock knock.
Who's there?
Interrupting cow.
Interrupting c—
MOO!!!

Q: Why do cows wear bells?
A: Because their horns don't work.

Q: What is the easiest way to count a herd of cattle?
A: Use a cowculator.

Q: What's a cow's favorite vegetable?
A: A cowat.

Q: What do you call a cow with two legs?
A: Lean beef.

Q: What do you call cattle with a sense of humor?
A: Laughing stock.

Q: Why are cows the perfect audience for a comedian?
A: Because they are easily amoosed.

Q: Why can't you shock cows?
A: Because they've herd it all.

Q: Where do cows go on Friday night?
A: To the moovie theater.

 Knock knock.
Who's there?
Cows say.
Cows say who?
No, silly, cows say moo.

Q: What do you get when you cross a cow and a duck?
A: Milk and quackers.

Q: What to you call a grumpy cow?
A: Moody.

Q: What do you call a clever duck?
A: A wise quacker.

Duck Bar

A duck walks into a bar and orders a drink.

The bartender says, "We don't serve ducks here."

The duck says, "I'll pay you 20 dollars."

"Your money isn't good here."

"Then put it on my bill."

Q: What time does a duck wake up in the morning?
A: At the quack of dawn.

Q: Why did the sheep go to the movies?
A: To get some snaa-aa-acks.

Q: What do you call a sheep that is covered in chocolate?
A: A Hershey baa-er.

Sheep Ice

Phil and Will built a skating rink in the middle of a pasture. One day a shepherd leading his flock through the pasture decided to take a shortcut across the rink. The sheep, however, were afraid of the ice and wouldn't cross it. Desperate, the shepherd began tugging one of them to the other side.

"Look at that," remarked Phil to Will. "That guy is trying to pull the wool over our ice!"

Q: Where do sheep go to get their wool cut?
A: To the baa-ber.

Q: What do you get if you cross a sheep with a kangaroo?
A: A wooly jumper.

Q: What did the well-mannered sheep say to her friend at the field gate?
A: "After ewe."

Q: What kind of horse goes out only after dark?
A: A nightmare.

Q: How do you make a slow horse fast?
A: Stop feeding it.

Thank God!

A man needed a horse, so he went to a stable and picked one out. Before he left with the horse, the owner told him that it was a special horse. The trainer, a religious man, had trained the horse to go with the command "Thank God," and to stop with the command "Amen."

So the man left, and a few minutes later he dozed off on his horse. Hours later, he woke up to find that his horse was racing him toward the edge of a cliff. Just in time, he shouted, "Amen!" and the horse stopped a few inches from the edge. "Whew," said the man. "Thank God!"

Q: What has four legs, a tail and is black and white?
A: A horse in jail.

Q: What is the slowest horse in the world?
A: A clotheshorse.

Q: Why do people like living next to ranches?
A: Because horses make good neigh-bors.

Q: How is a horse like a wedding?
A: They both need a groom.

Q: What did the horse say when it fell over?
A: "Help! I've fallen and I can't giddy up."

Q: Why couldn't the pony sing?
A: Because he was a little horse.

Q: What do pigs get when they're ill?
A: Oinkment.

Q: What do you get if you cross
a pig with a teddy bear?
A: A teddy boar.

Q: What do you call a pig
who plays basketball?
A: A ball hog.

Q: What do you call a pig that knows karate?
A: A pork chop.

Q: Where does a woodsman keep his pigs?
A: In a hog cabin.

Q: Why do pigs never recover from illness?
A: Because you have to kill them before you can cure them.

Q: What do you call a pig thief?
A: A ham burgler.

Q: What do you call a pig who's been arrested for dangerous driving?
A: A road hog.

Q: What do you call pigs that live together?
A: Pen pals.

Q: Why did the turkey cross the road twice?
A: To prove he wasn't chicken.

Q: Why didn't the chicken cross the road?
A: Because he was too chicken.

Q: Why did half a chicken cross the road?
A: To get to his other side.

Q: Why did the chewing gum cross the road?
A: Because it was stuck to the chicken's foot.

Q: Why did the chicken go to the seance?
A: To get to the other side.

Q: Why did the chicken cross the road, roll in mud and then cross the road again?
A: Because he was a dirty double-crosser.

Farm Boy

The farmer's son was returning from the market with the crate of chickens his father had entrusted to him, when all of a sudden he dropped the box and the door sprang open. Chickens scurried off in different directions, but the determined boy walked all over the neighborhood scooping up the wayward birds and returning them to the crate. Hoping he had found them all, the boy reluctantly returned home, expecting the worst.

"Pa, the chickens got loose," the boy confessed, "but I managed to find 12 of them."

"Well, you did real good, son," the farmer beamed. "You left with seven."

Q: What did the baby chick say when he saw his mother sitting on an orange?
A: "Dad, look what marma-laid!"

Q: What do you call a chicken in a shell suit?
A: An egg.

Q: Which side of a chicken has the most feathers?
A: The outside.

Q: Why do hens lay eggs?
A: Because if they dropped them, they'd break.

Q: What does a mixed-up hen lay?
A: Scrambled eggs.

Q: What does an evil hen lay?
A: Deviled eggs.

Q: How do chickens bake a cake?
A: From scratch.

Q: Why can't a rooster get rich?
A: Because he works for chicken feed.

A Two-part Joke

Q: What do you call a rooster that wakes you up every day?
A: An alarm cluck.

Q: What does an alarm cluck say?
A: Tick-tock-a-doodle-doo.

Q: What is the most musical part of a chicken?
A: The drumstick.

Q: What happened when the turkey got into a fight?
A: He got the stuffing knocked out of him.

Q: If fruit comes from a fruit tree, where does chicken come from?
A: A poul-tree.

Q: What do you call a haunted chicken?
A: A poultry-geist.

Q: What did the sick chicken say?
A: "Oh no! I have the people pox!"

Q: What do you call a crazy chicken?
A: A cuckoo cluck.

Q: What do you say when it rains chickens and ducks?
A: "What fowl weather!"

Q: What do you get if you cross a chicken with a cow?
A: Roost beef.

Q: Why does a chicken coop have two doors?
A: Because if it had four doors, it would be a chicken sedan.

Q: What did the llama say when he got kicked off the farm?
A: "Alpaca my bags."

feathered funnies

Q: How do you cure a sick bird?
A: Give it some tweetment.

Q: Why do birds fly south for the winter?
A: Because it's too far to walk.

Knock knock.
Who's there?
Owls say.
Owls say who?
Yep.

Q: What animal needs to wear a wig?
A: A bald eagle.

Q: What's the difference between a fly and a bird?
A: A bird can fly, but a fly can't bird.

Q: What kind of bird can lift the most weight?
A: A crane.

Q: What kind of bird is noisier than a whooping crane?
A: A trumpeter swan.

Q: What kind of bird is always sad?
A: A blue jay.

Q: What kind of bird is always out of breath?
A: A puffin.

Q: What do you get when you cross a high chair and a bird?
A: A stool pigeon.

Q: Why do seagulls fly over the sea?
A: Because if they flew over the bay, they'd be bagels.

Q: Why do hummingbirds hum?
A: Because they don't know the words.

Q: What do you call a woodpecker with no beak?
A: A headbanger.

Q: Why did the owl howl?
A: Because the woodpecker would peck her.

Knock knock.
Who's there?
Hoo.
Hoo who?
You sound like an owl.

Q: What is an owl's favorite subject in school?
A: Owl-gebra.

Q: Why do penguins wash their clothes in Tide?
A: Because it's too cold out-tide.

Q: What do penguins eat for lunch?
A: Ice berg-ers.

Q: Who is the penguin's favorite aunt?
A: Aunt Arctica.

- Someone said you sounded like an owl.
- Who?

Q: What do penguins sing at birthday parties?
A: "Freeze a Jolly Good Fellow."

Q: How does a penguin build its house?
A: Igloos it together.

In the Wild

Q: What is a bear's favorite phone?
A: A Blackberry.

Q: What do you call a toothless bear?
A: A gummy bear.

Q: Why did the deer need braces?
A: Because he had buck teeth.

Q: What did the buffalo say to his son when he left for college?
A: "Bison."

Q: What is the difference between a coyote and a flea?
A: One howls on the prairie and the other prowls on the hairy.

Q: What's black and white and makes a lot of noise?
A: A zebra with a drum kit.

Q: Why don't you see any giraffes in elementary school?
A: Because they're all in high school.

Knock knock.
Who's there?
Gorilla.
Gorilla who?
Gorilla me a hamburger. I'm hungry!

Q: What did the monkey say to his little brother?
A: "You're driving me bananas!"

Q: What kind of key opens a banana?
A: A monkey.

Q: How do you get down off an elephant?
A: You don't; you get down off a duck.

Q: What's big and gray with horns?
A: An elephant marching band.

Q: What is as big as an elephant but weighs nothing?
A: An elephant's shadow.

Q: What's the difference between an African elephant and an Indian elephant?
A: About 3000 miles.

Q: Why don't elephants need suitcases?
A: Because they already have trunks.

The Elephant and the Turtle

An elephant was drinking out of a river when he spotted a turtle asleep on a log. So he ambled on over and kicked the turtle clear across the river.

"What did you do that for?" asked a passing giraffe who had seen the kick.

"Because I recognized it as the same turtle that took a nip out of my trunk 53 years ago."

"Wow, what a memory," commented the giraffe.

"Yes," said the elephant. "Turtle recall."

Q: How do elephants talk to each other long distance?
A: Using the elephone.

Q: What wears glass slippers and weighs over 4000 pounds?
A: Cinderelephant.

Q: What do you get when you cross a fish with an elephant?
A: Swimming trunks.

Q: Who lost a herd of elephants?
A: Big Bo Peep.

Q: What kind of animal should you never play cards with?
A: A cheetah.

Q: Why did the leopard wear a striped shirt?
A: So he wouldn't be spotted.

Q: Is it hard to spot a leopard?
A: No, they come that way.

Q: What steps do you take if a tiger is running toward you?
A: Big ones.

Q: Why didn't the boy believe the tiger?
A: He thought it was a lion.

Q: How do you stop a lion from charging?
A: Take away its credit cards.

Hungry Lion

A hungry lion was roaming through the jungle looking for something to eat. He came across two men. One was sitting under a tree reading a book; the other was typing away on his laptop. The lion quickly pounced on the man reading the book and devoured him. Even the king of the jungle knows that readers digest and writers cramp.

Simba was walking too slowly, so I told him to Mufasa.

Q: Why did the lion spit out the clown?
A: Because he tasted funny.

Q: Why do lions eat raw meat?
A: Because they don't know how to cook.

Tourist: Is it true that a lion won't attack you if you're holding a tree branch?
Safari Guide: That depends on how fast you can run while you're carrying it.

Q: What do you call a lazy baby kangaroo?
A: A pouch potato.

Q: Why do kangaroo moms hate it when it rains?
A: Because their joeys have to play inside.

Q: What kind of tiles can't you stick on walls?
A: Reptiles.

Q: Where to turtles go to buy new shells?
A: The hard-wear store.

Q: What is an alligator's favorite drink?
A: Gatorade.

Q: What do you call an alligator in a vest?
A: An invistigator.

Q: Why couldn't the snake talk?
A: Because it had a frog in its throat.

Q: What do you get when you cross a snake and a book?
A: Hissstory.

Q: What kind of snakes are good at doing sums?
A: Adders.

Q: Why are snakes hard to fool?
A: Because you can't pull their leg.

Q: What kind of medicine do you give a sick snake?
A: Asp-irin.

OOPS

A baby snake asked its mom, "Mommy, are we poisonous?"

The mother snake responded, "Yes, honey, but why do you want to know?"

The baby snake responded, "Because I just bit myself..."

Rabbit, Rodent and Rank Riddles

Q: What kind of trick can a rabbit do on a BMX bike?
A: A bunny hop.

Q: Where does a rabbit learn how to fly?
A: In the hare force.

Q: What game do rabbits like to play?
A: Hop scotch.

Q: Why did the bald guy put a rabbit on his head?
A: Because he wanted hare.

Q: What do you comb a rabbit with?
A: A hare brush.

Q: What do you call a rabbit with fleas?
A: Bugs Bunny.

Q: What do you call a rabbit comedian?
A: A funny bunny.

Q: What do you call 13 rabbits in a row, hopping backward?
A: A receding hareline.

Q: What is a rabbit's favorite dance style?
A: Hip-hop.

Q: What city has the largest rodent population?
A: Hamsterdam.

Q: Why was the mouse crying?
A: Because he found out his dad was a rat.

Q: What is a mouse's favorite game?
A: Hide and squeak.

Q: What did one hedgehog say to another?
A: "Stay away from my hedge!"

Q: What did the judge say when a skunk walked into the courtroom?
A: "Odor in the court!"

Q: What do you get when you cross a giant with a skunk?
A: A big stink.

- Have you heard the one about the skunk?
- No.
- Never mind, it really stinks.

Q: Why are skunks always poor?
A: Because they have only one scent.

Q: What's black and white, black and white, black and white?
A: A skunk rolling down a hill.

Froggy Fun

Q: Where do you get frog eggs?
A: At the spawn shop.

Q: What is a frog's favorite exercise?
A: Jumping jacks.

Q: What's a toad's favorite sweet?
A: Lollihops.

Q: What is a frog's favorite soda?
A: Croak-a-Cola.

Q: How did the frog die?
A: He simply croaked.

Q: Where do frogs leave their hats and coats?
A: In the croakroom.

Q: What do you get when you cross a frog with a dog?
A: A croaker spaniel.

Frog Loan

A frog went to get a loan at a bank. The loan officer's name was Ms. Patty Stack. When the frog told Ms. Stack that he wanted a loan, she asked if he had collateral.

He showed her something that, to her, looked like nothing more than a toy marble, and said, "This is what I have for collateral."

She took the marble and showed it to the bank president and said, "There's a frog out there who wants a loan, and this is what he has for collateral. Do you know what this is, and should I give him the loan?"

The bank president said, "Why, that's a nic-nac, Patty Stack; give that frog a loan."

Q: What do you call a frog spy?
A: A croak and dagger agent.

Q: When do you see the most frogs?
A: When it is froggy out.

Q: What do you call a mean amphibian?
A: A bully frog.

Q: Why did the toad become a lighthouse keeper?
A: Because he had his own frog horn.

Q: What happens when frogs park illegally?
A: They get toad.

Q: What do frogs wear on their feet?
A: Open-toad shoes.

Tell Me My Future

A lonely frog telephones the Psychic Hotline and asks what his future holds.

His Personal Psychic Advisor tells him, "You are going to meet a beautiful young girl who will want to know everything about you."

The frog is thrilled. "This is great! Will I meet her at a party?" he croaks.

"No," says the psychic. "You'll meet her in biology class."

Q: What kind of poles can swim?
A: Tadpoles.

Q: What does a robot frog say?
A: "Rib-bot" (said in your best robot voice).

Q: What do you say to a hitchhiking frog?
A: "Hop in."

Q: What did one frog say to another?
A: "Time's sure fun when you're having flies."

Frog Bar

A man went to a restaurant, sat down, and there was a frog at the table. He asked the amphibian what he had to eat, and the frog replied, "Riblets."

Bee Funny

Q: Why do bees have sticky hair?
A: Because they use honeycombs.

Q: Who is the bee's favorite singer?
A: Sting.

Q: What is the bee's favorite pop group?
A: The Bee Gees.

Q: What do you get if you cross a bee with a skunk?
A: An animal that stings and stinks.

Q: What does a queen bee do when she burps?
A: She issues a royal pardon.

Q: How does a queen bee get around her hive?
A: She's throne.

Q: What kind of bee continually drops things?
A: A fumble bee.

Q: What is smarter than a talking bird?
A: A spelling bee.

Q: What did the bee say to the flower?
A: "Hello, honey!"

Q: Why did the bee get married?
A: Because he found his honey.

Q: What's a bee's favorite flower?
A: A bee-gonia.

Q: What does a bee say before it stings you?
A: "This is going to hurt me a lot more than it hurts you."

Knock knock.
Who's there?
Honey bee.
Honey bee who?
Honey, be a dear and get me a soda.

Q: How do bees get to school?
A: By school buzz.

other Small critters

Q: Why did the fly sit on the stove?
A: He wanted to be home on the range.

Q: How did the police scare the bugs away?
A: They called for the S.W.A.T. team.

Q: Two flies are on a porch; which one is an actor?
A: The one on the screen.

Q: Five flies are in the kitchen; which one is the football player?
A: The one in the sugar bowl.

Q: Why was the mother firefly happy?
A: Because her children were so bright.

Q: Why did the grasshopper go to the doctor?
A: Because he felt jumpy.

Q: Why was the centipede late?
A: Because he was playing "This Little Piggy" with his baby sister.

Q: What do you get if you cross a centipede and a parrot?
A: A walkie-talkie.

Q: What kind of doctors are like spiders?
A: Spin doctors.

Q: What did the spider say when she broke her new web?
A: "Darn it!"

Q: What do you get if you cross a spider and an elephant?
A: I'm not sure, but if you see one walking across the ceiling, run before it collapses!

Q: What did the spider say to the fly?
A: "I'm getting married; do you want to come to the webbing?"

Q: What happened when the chef found a daddy long legs in the salad?
A: It became a daddy short legs.

Q: Why did the spider turn on the computer?
A: Because he wanted to go on his website.

Q: How do spiders communicate?
A: Through the world wide web.

Q: Why was the baby ant confused?
A: Because all of his uncles were ants.

Q: What is the biggest ant in the world?
A: An elephant.

Q: Two silk worms are in a race; who wins?
A: Neither; it's a tie.

Q: What is the best advice to give a worm?
A: Sleep late.

Q: What did the mother worm say to the boy worm when he was late?
A: "Where in earth have you been?"

Q: What do you call a snail in charge of a ship?
A: A snailer.

Q: What does a snail say when it's riding on a turtle's back?
A: "Wheeeeeee!"

Q: How do two snails fight?
A: They slug it out.

Robbed

A snail entered a police station and told an officer, "I just got mugged by two turtles. They beat me up and took all my money!"

The officer replied, "Why that's terrible. Did you get a good look at them?"

"No sir, it all happened so fast!"

Under the Sea

Q: Why do fish swim in salt water?
A: Because pepper makes them sneeze.

Two fish are in a tank. One looks at the other and says, "Do you know how to drive this thing?"

Q: Why are fish so smart?
A: Because they live in schools.

Q: What is the easiest way to catch a fish?
A: Have someone throw one at you.

Q: What kind of money do fishermen make?
A: Net profits.

Q: How do you confuse a fish?
A: Put it in a round fishbowl and tell it to go to the corner.

 If you think of a better fish pun, let minnow.

Q: What kind of fish goes well with peanut butter?
A: Jellyfish.

Q: How many tickles does it take to make an octopus laugh?
A: Tentacles.

Q: What kind of noise annoys an oyster?
A: A noisy noise annoys an oyster. (Try saying that three times fast!)

Q: What did the boy fish say to his girlfriend?
A: "Your plaice or mine?"

Q: What did the fish say when it swam into a concrete wall?
A: "Dam!"

Q: Where does seaweed look for a job?
A: In the "kelp-wanted" ads.

Q: Why is a fish easy to weigh?
A: Because it has its own scales.

Q: What is the most musical part of a fish?
A: The scales.

- Have you ever seen a catfish?
- No. How would it hold the fishing rod?

Q: Why are fish boots the warmest ones to wear?
A: Because they have electric 'eels.

Q: Why are dolphins cleverer than humans?
A: Within three hours they can train a man to stand at the side of a pool and feed them fish.

Q: How do fish shop online?
A: They use a credit cod.

Q: To whom do fish go to borrow money?
A: The loan shark.

Q: Where to fish keep their money?
A: In the riverbank.

Q: What is the strongest creature in the sea?
A: The mussel.

Q: Why did the mussel hide his iPad from his sister?
A: Because he was being shellfish.

Dinosaurs

Q: What do you call a sleeping dinosaur?
A: A dinosnore.

Q: How do you know if there is a dinosaur in your refrigerator?
A: The door won't shut.

Q: What dinosaur would Harry Potter be?
A: A dinosorcerer.

Q: How can you best raise a baby dinosaur?
A: With a crane.

Q: What did the dinosaur put on her steak?
A: Dinosauce.

Q: What kind of dinosaur drinks Earl Gray?
A: A T-Rex.

Q: What does a triceratops sit on?
A: Its tricera-bottom.

Q: What is the best thing to do if you see a Tyrannosaurus Rex?
A: Pray that it doesn't see you.

Q: What's the nickname for someone who put their right hand in the mouth of a T-Rex?
A: Lefty.

Q: What game does the brontosaurus like to play with humans?
A: Squash.

Q: Why did the dinosaur cross the road?
A: To eat the chickens on the other side.

Q: What do you call a paleontologist who sleeps all the time?
A: Lazy bones.

Chapter 3

Boys and Girls

Q: Why did the kid throw a bucket of water out the window?
A: He wanted to see a waterfall.

Q: Why did the kid throw a block of butter out the window?
A: He wanted to see a butterfly.

Q: Why did the kid cross the park?
A: To get to the other slide.

Q: Why did the kid sleep with a ruler?
A: To measure how long he slept.

Q: Why was the kid running circles around his bed?
A: He wanted to catch up on his sleep.

How Do You Say?

Two sixth-graders waiting for the bus are discussing whether the composer Wagner is pronounced with a "W" sound or a "V" sound. So they stand there arguing and arguing, until they decide to ask a person who is walking by. One kid says to the gentleman, "Excuse me sir, is the composer Wagner pronounced 'Wagner' or 'Vagner'?"

The gentleman says, "Vagner."

As the gentleman is leaving, one kid says to him, "Thank you."

The gentleman replies, "You're velcome!"

Canadian kid: I was born in Canada.
American kid: Which part?
Canadian kid: All of me.

- Have you heard the story of the germ?
- No.
- Never mind, it'll spread.

Q: Why didn't the boy die when he drank some poison?
A: Because he was in the living room.

Q: Why did the boy take a pencil to bed?
A: To draw the curtains.

Mmmm, Marshmallow

One night a boy was sleeping and dreaming about eating a marshmallow, and when he woke up, his pillow was gone!

Text Speak

A girl texted a question to her friend: "What does IDK mean?"

Her friend texted back: "I don't know."

And the girl's response: "OMG!!! No one else does, either!"

Q: Why did the boy put paper over the TV?
A: He was trying to make paper view.

Q: Why did the girl sleep under the car?
A: Because she wanted to wake up oily.

Girl: Do you know what really amazes me about you?
Boy: No. What?
Girl: Oops. Sorry. I was thinking about someone else!

Q: Why were boys created before girls?
A: Because you always need a rough draft before the final copy.

Anna: Tom says I'm pretty. Andy says I'm ugly. What do you think, Jason?
Jason: I think you're pretty ugly.

Q: Why did the boy take a prune to the movie theater?
A: Because he couldn't find a date.

Bully Burn

I got in a fight one time with a really big tough guy who said, "I'm going to mop the floor with your face."

I said, "You'll be sorry."

He said, "Oh, yeah? Why?"

I said, "Well, you won't be able to get into the corners very well."

Idiots

Two teenage boys are walking down the street when one of them sees a broken piece of mirror on the ground, grabs it, looks at it and says, "This guy looks so familiar, but I can't remember where I know him from."

The other guy grabs it from his hand, takes a look at it and says, "It's me, you idiot!"

True Love

Just before going in for heart surgery, a girl says to her boyfriend, "I love you!"

The boy says, "I love you more, much much more!"

After the surgery, when the girl woke up, only her father is next to her bed. The girl says, "Where is my boyfriend?"

Her father responds, "You don't know who gave you the heart?"

The girl says, "What?!" and starts crying.

Her father says, "I'm just kidding. He went to the bathroom."

Stranded

Three girls stranded on a desert island find a magic lantern containing a genie who grants them each one wish. The brunette girl wishes she was off the island and back home. The red-headed girl wishes the same. The blonde girl says, "I'm lonely. I wish my friends were back here."

Q: Why did the girl bring lipstick and eye shadow to school?
A: Because she had a make-up exam.

Q: Why did the boy bury his flashlight?
A: Because the batteries died.

Knowledge

Two kindergarten kids are talking during their lunch break.

Girl: What is the capital of America?
Boy: Washington, D. C.
Girl: No, it's not! "A" is the capital of America.

Lincoln Burn

A father said to his son, "When Abe Lincoln was your age, he was studying books by the light of the fireplace."

The son replied, "When Lincoln was your age, he was President."

Smart Lad

Two old guys are sitting on the one man's front porch when a couple of kids come out of the house next door and start walking by. The one old man says to his friend, "The kid who lives there is the dumbest kid in the world. Watch while I prove it to you."

The old guy puts a dollar bill in one hand and two quarters in the other, then calls his neighbor boy over and asks, "Which do you want, son?"

The boy takes the quarters, thanks the man and leaves.

"What did I tell you?" says the man to his friend. "That kid never learns!"

Later, when the boys are out of ear shot of the two old guys, the one boy asks his friend, "Why did you take the quarters instead of the dollar bill?"

He replies, "Because the day I take the dollar, the game is over!"

Two dudes walk into a bar. The third one ducks.

Q: What is mom and dad's favorite ride at a fair?
A: A married-go-round!

Q: What kind of stories do ship captains' children like to hear?
A: Ferry tales.

Helping Dad

A clergyman walking down a country lane sees a young farmer struggling to load hay back onto a cart after it had fallen off.

"You look hot, my son," said the cleric. "Why don't you rest a moment, and I'll give you a hand."

"No thanks," said the young man. "My father wouldn't like it."

"Don't be silly," the minister said. "Everyone is entitled to a break. Come and have a drink of water."

Again the young man protested that his father would be upset.

Losing his patience, the clergyman said, "Your father must be a real slave driver. Tell me where I can find him and I'll give him a piece of my mind!"

"Well," replied the young farmer, "he's under the load of hay."

Babies

A young boy asked his mother where babies come from and she answered, "Go ask your father."

He asked his father the same question and he answered, "Go ask your mother."

Later that day at dinner, the boy announced, "I know that I am not your son because neither one you knows where babies come from."

out!

A prisoner, after many years, is finally released from jail. He runs around yelling, "I'm free! I'm free!"

A boy sent ten different puns to friends, in hope that at least one of the puns would make them laugh. Unfortunately, no pun in ten did.

A little kid walks up to him and says, "So what? I'm four."

Supper Time Part 1

Johnny: Dad, are caterpillars good to eat?
Father: What have I told you about inappropriate dinnertime conversation?
Mother: Why did you say that, Johnny? Why did you ask the question?
Johnny: Because I saw one on Dad's lettuce, but now it's gone.

Supper Time Part 2

Johnny: Today in the park I was surrounded by lions!
Father: Now, Johnny, what have we told you about telling tales?
Johnny: I'm not lying; I was surrounded by hundreds of lions—dandelions!

Thou Shalt Not!

A Sunday school teacher was discussing the Ten Commandments with her five- and six-year-olds. After explaining the commandment to "Honor thy father and thy mother," she asked, "Is there a commandment that teaches us how to treat our brothers and sisters?"

Without missing a beat, one little boy answered, "Thou shalt not kill."

Sunday School

A Sunday school teacher said to her class, "We have been learning how powerful kings and queens were in Bible times. But, there is a higher power. Can anybody tell me what it is?"

One mischievous child called out, "Aces!"

Be Like Jesus

Seeing her two sons fighting over the last piece of pizza, the mother said, "You boys should be acting more like Jesus. If he were here, he would give his brother the last piece."

The older brother looked at his younger sibling and said, "Marty, you be Jesus."

Q: Why did Eve want to move to New York?
A: She fell for the Big Apple.

Q: What kind of lighting did Noah use for the ark?
A: Floodlights.

Q: Who built the ark?
A: I have Noah idea!

Perfect Understanding

A 10-year-old boy was attending his first wedding. After the service, his cousin asked him, "How many women can a man marry?"

"Sixteen," the boy responded.

His cousin was amazed that he had an answer so quickly. "How do you know that?"

"Easy," the little boy said. "All you have to do is add it up, like the minister said: four better, four worse, four richer, four poorer."

Q: Why did the boy sit on a pumpkin?
A: Because he wanted to play squash.

Police arrested two kids yesterday; one was drinking battery acid, and the other was eating fireworks. They charged one, and they let the other one off.

Q: Why was the girl suspicious of the ocean?
A: Because there was something fishy about it.

Brothers

Mrs. Jones, mother of two, was observing her children playing in the snow. She called the oldest one inside to speak to him. "Bobby, I told you to share your toys with your brother."

"I am sharing, Mom. He plays with the sled going up the hill, and I play with it going down."

Q: What do you call a bunch of Barbies standing in line?
A: A Barbie queue.

Q: What happened when the boy took the train home?
A: His mother made him bring it back.

Q: Why shouldn't you shower with a Pokemon around?
A: It might Pikachu.

Water Daddy!

A boy was in trouble, so he got sent to bed early. He got in bed and asked his dad for a glass of water, so his dad brought him a glass.

Five minutes later the boy called down too his dad, "Can I have another glass of water?"

His dad said, "No, you've had enough water. Go to sleep."

Five minutes later the boy called back down to his dad saying, "Can I PLEASE have another glass of water?"

His dad said, "NO, and if you ask me one more time, I'm going to come up there and spank you."

So the boy called down, "On your way up to spank me, can you bring me a glass of water?"

Things My Mother is Teaching Me

1. My mother is teaching me ANTICIPATION: "Just wait until your father gets home."

2. My mother is teaching me about RECEIVING: "You're going to get it when we get home!"

3. My mother is teaching me to MEET A CHALLENGE: "What were you thinking? Answer me when I talk to you! Don't talk back to me!"

4. My mother is teaching me LOGIC: "If you fall out off that swing and break your neck, you're not coming to the store with me."

5. My mother is teaching me MEDICAL SCIENCE: "If you don't stop crossing your eyes, they are going to freeze that way."

6. My mother is teaching me to THINK AHEAD: "If you don't pass your spelling test, you'll never get a good job."

7. My mother is teaching me HUMOR: "When that lawn mower cuts off your toes, don't come running to me."

8. My mother is teaching me how to BECOME AN ADULT: "If you don't eat your vegetables, you'll never grow up."

9. My mother is teaching me about GENETICS: "You're just like your father."

10. My mother is teaching me about my ROOTS: "Do you think you were born in a barn?"

11. My mother is teaching me the WISDOM OF AGE: "When you get to be my age, you'll understand."

And last but not least...

12. My mother is teaching me about JUSTICE: "One day you'll have kids, and I hope they turn out just like you; then you'll see what it's like!"

Boys and Girls at the Door

Knock knock.
Who's there?
Bob.
Bob who?
I do not know his last
    name.

Knock knock.
Who's there?
Doris.
Doris who?
Doris locked. That's why
    I'm knocking.

Knock knock.
Who's there?
Leena.
Leena who?
Leena little closer, and I will
    tell you.

Knock knock.
Who's there?
Kareem.
Kareem who?
Kareem of the crop.

Knock knock.
Who's there?
Wendy.
Wendy who?
Wendy wind blows,
    de cradle will rock.

Knock knock.
Who's there?
Dwayne.
Dwayne who?
Dwayne the tub,
    I'm dwowning!

Knock knock.
Who's there?
Al.
Al who?
Al give you a kiss if you open
   this door.

Knock knock.
Who's there?
Drew.
Drew who?
Drew you know the time?

Knock knock.
Who's there?
Justin.
Justin who?
Justin case you forgot,
   I'm still out here.

Knock knock.
Who's there?
Anita.
Anita who?
Anita tissue—ah-choo!

Knock knock.
Who's there?
Jimmy.
Jimmy who?
Jimmy some food,
   I'm starving.

Knock knock.
Who's there?
Alex.
Alex who?
Alex-plain later,
   just let me in!

Chapter 4

Fun with Food

Q: What did one plate say to the other?
A: "Dinner's on me."

Customer: Waiter, this food tastes kind of funny.
Waiter: Then why aren't you laughing?

Q: What makes the leaning Tower of Pisa lean?
A: It doesn't eat much.

Q: What color is a hiccup?
A: Burple.

Q: How do you fix a broken pizza?
A: With tomato paste.

Customer: Waiter, will my pizza be long?
Water: No, sir, it will be round.

Milk It

Did you hear about the mad scientist who put dynamite in his fridge? They say he blew his cool!

Q: How can you delay milk turning sour?
A: Keep it in the cow.

Q: What is white, has a horn and gives milk?
A: A dairy truck.

Q: What kind of cheese isn't yours?
A: Nacho cheese.

Q: How do you make a milkshake?
A: Give it a good scare.

Q: What cheese is made backwards?
A: Edam.

Q: How do you make a cheese puff?
A: Chase it around the kitchen.

Grain Groaners

Q: Why won't you starve in a desert?
A: Because of all the sand which is there.

Q: What do elves make sandwiches with?
A: Shortbread.

Q: What is a pretzel's favorite dance?
A: The Twist.

Q: What is a cheerleader's favorite food?
A: Cheerios.

Q: What do snowmen eat for breakfast?
A: Frosted Flakes.

Q: What do you call a noodle that committed identity theft?
A: An im-pasta.

Q: Why did the woman take a bag of oats to bed with her?
A: To feed her nightmare.

Fruit Punch-lines

Q: How do you make fruit punch?
A: Give it boxing lessons.

Q: What happened to the overturned fruit truck?
A: It caused a big traffic jam.

Q: When do you go on red and stop on green?
A: When you're eating watermelon.

Q: What did the grape say when it got stepped on?
A: Nothing, it just let out a little wine.

Q: Why do melons get married in church?
A: Because they cantaloupe.

Q: What's worse than finding a worm in your apple?
A: Taking a bite and finding a half a worm in your apple.

Q: What are twins' favorite fruit?
A: Pears.

Time flies like an arrow. Fruit flies like a banana.

Q: What do you give to a sick lemon?
A: Lemon aid.

Q: What is a scarecrow's favorite fruit?
A: Strawberries.

Q: What is a ghost's favorite fruit?
A: BOO! berries.

Q: What do you call a sad strawberry?
A: A blueberry.

Q: Why did the strawberry call for help?
A: Because its mama was in a jam.

Q: What is Beethoven's favorite fruit?
A: Ba-na-na-NAAA.

Knock knock.
Who's there?
Figs.
Figs who?
Figs the doorbell, it's broken.

Q: If a crocodile makes shoes, what does a banana make?
A: Slippers.

Q: What are two banana peels together called?
A: A pair of slippers.

Q: What does one banana say to the other banana?
A: "Keep your eyes peeled."

Q: Why did the banana go to the doctor?
A: Because it wasn't peeling well.

Knock knock.
Who's there?
Banana.
Banana who?
Knock knock.
Who's there?
Banana.
Banana who?
Knock knock.
Who's there?
Banana.
Banana who?
Knock knock.
Who's there?
Orange.
Orange who?
Orange you glad I didn't say banana?

Q: Why didn't the banana snore?
A: Because it didn't want to wake up the rest of the bunch.

Witty Veggies

Q: What do nosy peppers do?
A: They get jalapeño business.

Q: How do you turn soup into gold?
A: Add 24 carrots.

Q: Why was the soup so expensive?
A: Because it had 24 carrots.

What?

When the waitress in a restaurant brought her customer the soup du jour, the man was dismayed. "Good heavens," he said. "What is this?"

"Why, it's bean soup," she replied.

"I don't care what it has been," he sputtered. "What is it now?"

Q: Why did the cucumber blush?
A: Because it saw the salad dressing.

Q: What is the worst vegetable to serve on a boat?
A: Leek.

Knock knock.
Who's there?
Olive.
Olive who?
I love you, too!

Q: What is green and sings?
A: Britney Spearagus.

FUN WITH FOOD

Q: What is green and sings?
A: Elvis Parsley.

Q: How does Lady Gaga like her vegetables?
A: Raw, raw, ra-ra-rawwww!

Q: What did one tomato say to the other?
A: "You go on ahead; I'll ketchup!"

Family Time

A family of three tomatoes was walking downtown one day when the baby tomato started lagging behind. The father tomato walked back to the baby tomato and stomped on her, squashing her into a red paste, and said, "Ketchup!"

Q: Why is a tomato round and red?
A: Because if it was long and green it would be a cucumber.

Q: What is black, white, green and bumpy?
A: A pickle wearing a tuxedo.

Knock knock.
Who's there?
Ketchup.
Ketchup who?
Ketchup to me, and I will tell you.

Q: How do you divide 20 potatoes among six people?
A: Boil them and mash them.

Q: Why shouldn't you tell a secret on a farm?
A: Because the potatoes have eyes and the corn has ears.

Q: What did the baby corn say to the mama corn?
A: "Where's pop corn?"

Q: What type of room has nothing in it?
A: A mushroom.

Mushroom

A mushroom walks into a bar and asks for a drink. The bartender says, "We don't serve your kind in here!"

The mushroom says, "Why not? I'm a fun-gi!"

Protein Puns

Q: Why did the egg go to the doctor?
A: Because it had a cracking headache.

Q: How do you make an egg laugh?
A: Tell it a yolk.

Q: Why shouldn't you tell an egg a joke?
A: Because it might crack up.

Mother: Would you like a duck egg for breakfast?
Son: Only if you quack it for me.

Sausages

Two sausages are frying in a pan. One sausage turns to the other sausage and says, "Boy, it's hot in here."

The other sausage turns and says, "Holy crap, a talking sausage!"

Q: Why do the French like to eat snails?
A: Because they don't like fast food!

Q: What kind of nut always seems to have a cold?
A: A cashew.

Q: What do you call an almond in a spacesuit?
A: An astronut.

Knock knock.
Who's there?
Cash.
Cash who?
No thank you, but I'll take a peanut.

Q: How do you make a walnut laugh?
A: Crack it up.

Silly Sweets

Q: Why did the Oreo go to the dentist?
A: Because it lost its filling.

Q: When is a door sweet and tasty?
A: When it's jammed.

Q: Why did the cookie go to the doctor?
A: Because it felt crummy.

Q: What is the farmer's favorite candy?
A: Jolly Ranchers.

Q: In which school do you learn to make ice cream?
A: Sundae school.

Q: What's the best thing to put into a pie?
A: Your teeth.

Q: Why did the Jellybean go to school?
A: Because he wanted to be a Smartie.

Q: What do you call cocoa that was stolen?
A: Hot chocolate.

Q: What candy do you eat on the playground?
A: Recess pieces.

Q: Why did the lady love to drink hot chocolate?
A: Because she was a cocoa-nut!

Q: What kind of keys do kids like to carry?
A: Cookies.

Q: Why don't they serve chocolate in prison?
A: Because it makes you break out.

- Did you hear the joke about the peanut butter?
- No.
- Well I'm not telling you. You might spread it!

 Knock knock.
Who's there?
Doughnut.
Doughnut who?
Doughnut worry, it's just a joke.

Chapter 5

Weird and Wacky

Q: What has a head and a tail, but no body?
A: A coin.

Q: Why did the penny jump off the building and the dime didn't?
A: Because the dime had more cents.

Q: Where can you always find money?
A: In the dictionary.

Q: Why did Superman cross the road?
A: To get to the supermarket.

Q: What did Batman and Robin become after they got run over by a steamroller?
A: Flatman and Ribbon.

Q: How did the man become Thor?
A: He forgot to thtretch.

Q: Why is Peter Pan always flying?
A: Because he Neverlands.

Q: Why did the leprechaun iron his four-leaf clover?
A: Because he wanted to press his luck.

Kiss the Frog

A 92-year-old man is walking through a park and comes across a talking frog.

The frog says, "If you kiss me, I will turn into a beautiful princess and be yours for a week."

The old man picks up the frog and puts it in his pocket.

The frog screams, "Hey! If you kiss me, I will turn into a beautiful princess and be yours for the rest of your life!"

The old man says, "I'd rather have a talking frog."

Q: Why did Mozart get rid of his chickens?
A: Because they kept saying, "Bach, Bach, Bach."

Q: What do you call four bullfighters in quicksand?
A: Cuatro sink-o.

Q: What do you do when you break your big toe?
A: Call a Big Toe Truck.

Q: Who is the one celebrity that arm wrestlers don't want to meet?
A: Neil Armstrong.

Q: What do you call someone with no body and no nose?
A: Nobody knows.

Q: Why can't your nose be 12 inches long?
A: Because then it would be a foot.

Q: What did one eye say to the other?
A: "Between you and me, something smells."

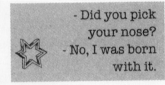
- Did you pick your nose?
- No, I was born with it.

Q: What has a bottom at the top?
A: Your legs.

Q: What is the most musical bone?
A: The trombone.

Q: What was the pessimist's blood type?
A: B negative.

Archery

Once upon a time there was an archery contest.

The first archer, wearing cape and a mask covering his face, lines up in position. He fires an arrow, which finds the center of the target. Then he takes off his mask and shouts, "I am Robin Hood!" The crowd cheers.

The second archer, also in disguise, lines up in position. He fires his arrow, which hits the center and splits Robin Hood's arrow in two! He takes off his mask and shouts, "I am William Tell!" The crowd cheers.

Finally, a third masked man lines up in position. He fires his arrow, but it goes all wrong—it flies past the target and kills the king! Then the man takes off his mask and shouts, "I am...sorry!"

Q: Why did Robin Hood rob only the rich?
A: Because the poor didn't have anything worth stealing.

Q: What did the Sheriff of Nottingham say when Robin Hood fired at him?
A: "That was an arrow escape!"

Do You Believe in Magic?

A magician worked on a cruise ship in the Caribbean. The audience would be different each week, so the magician did the same tricks each week. However, there was a problem: the captain's parrot saw the shows each week and began to understand how the magician did every trick. Once he understood, he started shouting out the secrets in the middle of the show. "Look, it's not the same hat." "Look, he's hiding the flowers under the table." "Hey, why are all the cards the Ace of Spades?"

The magician was furious, but he couldn't do anything—it was, after all, the captain's parrot. One day, the ship had an accident and sank. The magician found himself with the parrot, adrift on a piece of wood in the middle of the sea. They stared at each other with hatred, but neither one uttered a word. This went on for a day, then another, and another. Finally, after a week, the parrot said, "Okay, I give up. Where the heck is the boat?"

Q: Why was the clown sad?
A: Because he broke his funny bone.

I went to the bank the other day and asked the teller to check my balance, so she pushed me!

Q: Where do fortune tellers go to dance?
A: The crystal ball.

Q: Why didn't the acrobat work in winter?
A: Because he only wanted to do summer-saults.

Cowboy Up

A cowboy rides his horse into town to attend a meeting. As he is about to head back home, he notices that his horse is missing. He shouts, "If I don't find my horse, I will do exactly what I did when I lost my first horse!" Suddenly, the horse appears.

Out of curiosity, a man goes up to the cowboy and asks, "What did you do when you lost your first horse?"

"I walked."

Q: What did the cowboy say when the bear ate Lassie?
A: "Well, doggone!"

Q: How much do pirates pay to get their ears pierced?
A: A buccaneer.

Q: What is a pirate's favorite letter of the alphabet?
A: You'd think it would be the R, but it's the C.

Q: Why did it take the pirate so long to memorize the alphabet?
A: Because he always got lost at C.

Q: Why couldn't the pirate play cards?
A: Because he was sitting on the deck.

Q: Why are pirates such great singers?
A: Because they can hit the high C's.

Q: What geometric figure is like a lost parrot?
A: A polygon.

Boy: Pete and Repete are sitting in a boat. Pete falls out. Who's left in the boat?
Girl: Repete.
Boy: Okay, but pay attention this time. Pete and Repete are sitting...

Sherlock

Sherlock Holmes and Dr. Watson went on a camping trip. After a good meal and a bottle of wine, they laid down for the night and went to sleep. Some hours later, Holmes awoke and nudged his faithful friend. "Watson, look up at the sky and tell me what you see."

Watson replied, "I see millions and millions of stars."

"What does that tell you?" asked Holmes.

Watson pondered for a minute. "Astronomically, it tells me that there are millions of galaxies, and potentially billions of planets. Astrologically, I observe that Saturn is in Leo. Horologically, I deduce that the time is approximately a quarter past three. Theologically, I can see that God is all powerful and that we are small and insignificant. Meteorologically, I suspect that we will have a beautiful day tomorrow. What does it tell you?"

Holmes was silent for a minute, then spoke: "It tells me that someone has stolen our tent."

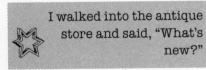

I walked into the antique store and said, "What's new?"

Q: What is the shortest month?
A: May. It has only three letters.

Q: How many seconds there are in a year?
A: Twelve—January 2nd, February 2nd...

Q: Why was everyone so tired on April 1?
A: Because they had just finished a March of 31 days.

WEIRD AND WACKY

Q: If April showers bring May flowers, what do May flowers bring?
A: Pilgrims.

> Did you hear about the paddle sale at the boat store? It was quite an oar deal.

Q: What happened to the thief who stole a calendar?
A: He got 12 months.

Q: Why did the robber take a bath?
A: Because he wanted to make a clean getaway.

Q: What did one elevator say to the other?
A: "I think I'm coming down with something."

Q: What did the stamp say to the envelope?
A: "Stick with me, and we'll go places."

Q: What type of music are balloons afraid of?
A: Pop music.

Q: What has four wheels and flies?
A: A garbage truck.

Q: What rock group has four guys who can't sing?
A: Mount Rushmore.

Q: Why did the traffic light turn red?
A: Because it had to change in the middle of the street.

Q: What do you get if you cross a chili pepper, a shovel and a chihuahua?
A: A hot-diggity-dog.

Patient: I keep having nightmares about monsters under my bed. I'm exhausted. What can I do?
Doctor: Saw the legs off your bed.

Patient: I keep on seeing an insect spinning in circles.
Doctor: Don't worry, it's just a bug that's going around.

Patient: I swallowed a lot of food coloring.
Doctor: Don't worry, you'll be okay.
Patient: But I feel like I've dyed a little inside.

Patient: I think I'm losing my memory.
Doctor: When did it start?
Patient: When did what start?

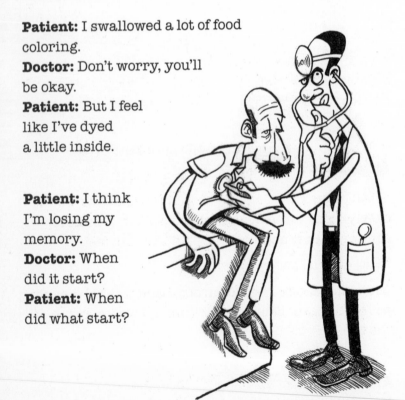

Patient: I feel like everyone is ignoring me.
Doctor: Next!

Patient: I feel like a pony.
Doctor: Don't worry, you're just a little hoarse.

Patient: I think I'm a pair of curtains.
Doctor: Pull yourself together.

Patient: Doctor, I think I need glasses!
Waiter: You certainly do—this is a restaurant!

Brave Man

A tour guide was talking with a group of school kids at Yellowstone park when one of the kids asked him if he had ever come face-to-face with a wolf.

"Yes, I came face-to-face with a wolf once. And as luck would have it, I was alone and without a weapon."

"What did you do?" the little girl asked.

"First, I tried looking him straight in the eyes, but he slowly came toward me. I moved back, but he kept coming nearer and nearer. I had to think fast."

"How did you get away?"

"As a last resort, I turned around and walked quickly out of the cage. That was back when I was working at the zoo."

Q: What do lawyers wear to court?
A: Lawsuits.

Q: Why did the archaeologist decide on a career change?
A: Because his career was in ruins.

Q: What do you call a carpenter who loses his tools?
A: A saw loser.

Q: Why did the librarian keep reading the book on anti-gravity?
A: Because it was impossible to put down.

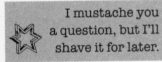
- Wanna hear a construction joke?
- Sure, I'd love to hear a construction joke.
- Sorry, I'm still working on it!

Q: Why did the man lose his job at the orange juice factory?
A: Because he couldn't concentrate.

Q: Why did the man lose his job at the calendar factory?
A: Because he took a day off.

Q: Why did the policeman go to the baseball game?
A: Because he heard someone had stolen a base.

I mustache you a question, but I'll shave it for later.

Customer: I want a haircut, please.
Barber: Certainly. Which one?

Q: How did the barber win the race?
A: He knew a shortcut.

Monstrous Jokes

Q: What do you get when you cross a snowman with a vampire?
A: Frostbite.

Vampire Competition

Once upon a time, three vampires met. Each one of them was boasting about their vampiric abilities.

Vampire A said, "Look at that mansion over there! I can finish all of its inhabitants within 10 minutes!"

And so he flew to the mansion, and nine minutes later, he came back with his mouth filled with blood, looking satisfied with himself.

Vampire B then said, "Bah! Look at that village over there! Give me five minutes!"

He flew to the village, and five minutes later he was back, his mouth dripping red blood.

Vampire C then said, "Pffft! Look at the TOWN over there! Give me three minutes!"

He flew in the direction of the town, and one minute later, he returned with his mouth filled with blood.

Vampires A and B were amazed. They asked, "How do you have such speed, friend?"

Vampire C pointed, then asked them, "Do you see that building over there?"

"Yes!" answered A and B.

"Well I did not!"

Q: Where do you wash a vampire?
A: In the bat room.

Q: Why do vampires brush their teeth?
A: To stop bat breath.

Q: What kind of medicine does Dracula take for a cold?
A: Coffin medicine.

Q: What is Dracula's favorite coffee?
A: Decoffinated.

Q: What do you get if you cross Dracula with Sir Lancelot?
A: A bite in shining armor.

Q: What is Dracula's favorite fruit?
A: Blood oranges.

Q: What breed of dog does Dracula have?
A: A bloodhound.

Q: Why are ghosts bad liars?
A: Because you can see right through them.

Q: What should a short-sighted ghost have?
A: Spooktacles.

WEIRD AND WACKY

Q: What kind of street does a ghost live on?
A: A dead end.

Q: Where do ghosts get an education?
A: At high sghoul.

Q: Why do ghosts make good cheerleaders?
A: Because they have a lot of spirit.

Q: What did the ghost say as it floated into the terrified girl's bedroom?
A: Don't worry, I'm just passing through.

Q: Which room in the house is useless to a ghost?
A: The living room.

 Knock knock.
Who's there?
Boo!
Boo who?
Don't cry, it's only me.

Q: Why didn't the skeleton cross the road?
A: He didn't have the guts.

Q: Why was the skeleton laughing?
A: Because of its funny bone.

Q: How do skeletons get their mail?
A: By bony express.

Q: How do you stop a werewolf from chasing you?
A: Throw a stick and say fetch.

Q: Why did the mummy leave his tomb after
3000 years?
A: Because he thought he was old enough to leave home.

Q: What is a mummy's favorite type of music?
A: Wrap music.

Q: Where do abominable snowmen go to dance?
A: To snowballs.

Q: Why didn't the zombie go to school?
A: Because he felt rotten.

Q: Why did the cyclops stop teaching?
A: Because he only had one pupil.

Q: What kind of witch is good to have around when
it's dark?
A: A lights witch.

Chapter 6

Shhh... Not for Your Parents

Q: Why did the blonde climb over the chain-link fence?
    A: To see what was on the other side.

Q: How do you drown a blonde?
    A: Put a scratch-and-sniff sticker on the bottom of the pool.

Escape from Jail

A blonde, a brunette and a redhead escaped from jail. Looking for a place to hide, all of them ran into a bar. The brunette hid behind a box, the redhead behind the door, and the blonde inside a potato sack. Soon the police came into the bar. One officer kicked the box; the brunette said, "Arf," so they thought it was a dog.

Next the police officer kicked the door; the redhead said, "Meow," so they thought it was a cat. Then the officer kicked the potato sack; the blonde said, "Potato!"

Swimmers

A blonde, brunette and redhead were standing on the edge of the pool ready for the 100 meter breast stroke race. The starter shot the pistol, and the three women dove into the water and began swimming.

> One blonde walks into a bar, then another blonde walks into a bar. The first blonde says, "You didn't see it either?"

Less than a minute later, the brunette finished and jumped out of the water. Then the redhead. About 20 minutes later, the blonde emerged.

They awarded the gold to the brunette, the silver to the redhead and the bronze to the blonde. As they placed the medal around her neck, the blonde whispered, "I don't want to sound like a sore loser, but I think the other two used their arms."

If Jane Was Blonde

Tarzan was tired when he came home.

"What have you been doing today?" asked Jane.

> A blonde invention: solar powered flashlight.

"Chasing a herd of elephants on vines," said Tarzan.

"Really?" said Jane. "I thought elephants stayed on the ground."

Ear Ache

One day a blonde walks into a doctor's office with both of her ears burnt. The doctor asks her what happened. She says, "I was doing my ironing when the phone rang, and I mistakenly picked up the iron instead of the phone."

"Well that explains one ear, but what about the other?"

"The phone rang again."

1. Say "eye."
2. Spell the word "map."
3. Say "ness."

Say What?!

As the storm raged, the captain realized his ship was sinking fast. He called out, "Anyone here know how to pray?"

One man stepped forward. "Aye, Captain, I know how to pray."

"Good," said the captain. "You pray while the rest of us put on our life jackets—we're one short."

 Knock knock.
Who's there?
Smell mop.
Smell mop who?

Q: How do crazy people go through the forest?
A: They take the psycho path.

Q: Where does the one-legged man work?
A: At IHOP.

Q: Why did the one-handed man cross the road?
A: To get to the secondhand shop.

cats

See if you can do this. Read each line aloud without making any mistakes. If you make a mistake, you MUST start over or it won't work.

This is this cat.
This is is cat.
This is how cat.
This is to cat.
This is keep cat.
This is a cat.
This is dummy cat.
This is busy cat.
This is for cat.
This is forty cat.
This is seconds cat.

Now go back and read the third word in each line from the top.

Q: What do you get if you cross a cat with a canary?
A: A peeping tom.

Q: What else do you get if you cross a cat with a canary?
A: Shredded tweet.

Hungry Cannibals

Two cannibals, a father and son, were elected by the tribe to go out and get something to eat. They walked deep into the jungle and waited by a path.

An elephant sees a man naked and asks, "How do you drink water with that?"

Before long, along came a little old man. The son said, "Oooh Dad, there's one."

"No," said the father. "There's not enough meat on that one to feed the dogs. We'll just wait."

A little while later, along came a really fat woman. The son said, "Hey Dad, she's plenty big enough."

"No," said the father. "We'd all die of a heart attack from the fat in that one. We'll just wait."

About an hour later, there came an absolutely gorgeous woman. The son said, "Now I know there's nothing wrong with that one, Dad. Let's eat her."

"No," said the father. "We'll not eat her either."

"Why not?" asked the son.

"Because we're going to take her back alive and eat your mother."

A dirty joke: the white horse fell in the mud.

Q: What happened to the cannibal who was late to dinner?
A: They gave her the cold shoulder.

Q: Why does a squirrel swim on his back?
A: To keep his nuts dry.

Top 20 Ways to Say Someone is Stupid

20. A few clowns short of a circus.

19. A few fries short of a Happy Meal.

18. A few peas short of a casserole.

17. Doesn't have all his Cornflakes in one box.

16. The wheel's spinning, but the hamster's dead.

15. One Fruit Loop shy of full bowl.

14. Body by Fisher, brains by Mattel.

13. Warning: Objects in mirror are dumber than they appear.

12. Couldn't pour water out of a boot with instructions on the heel.

11. Too much yardage between the goalposts.

10. An intellect rivaled only by garden tools.

9. As smart as bait.

8. Elevator doesn't go all the way to the top floor.

7. Antenna doesn't pick up all the channels.

6. Belt doesn't go through all the loops.

5. If he had another brain, it would be lonely.

4. Proof that evolution can go in reverse.

3. Receiver is off the hook.

2. Several nuts short of a full pouch.

1. Fell out of the stupid tree and hit every branch on the way down.

I got tasered picking up my friend from the airport today. Apparently security doesn't like it when you shout, "Hi, Jack!"

Q: Why did the rapper carry an umbrella?
A: Fo' drizzle.

Q: How many Emos does it take to screw in a light bulb?
A: None. They are all crying in the dark.

Q: How many real men does it take to change a light bulb?
A: None. Real men aren't afraid of the dark.

Step 1: Name your iPhone "Titanic."
Step 2: Plug it into your computer.
Step 3: When iTunes says "Titanic is syncing," press cancel.
Step 4: Feel like a hero.

A Puzzle

- Arnold Schwarzenegger has a big one.
- Michael J. Fox has a small one.
- Madonna doesn't have one.
- The Pope has one but doesn't use it.
- Bill Clinton uses his all the time.
- Mickey Mouse has an unusual one.
- George Burns' was hot.
- Liberace NEVER gave his to a woman.
- Jerry Seinfeld is very very proud of his.
- We never saw Lucy use Desi's.

Q: What is it?
A: A last name.

Chapter 7

A Few More Chuckles

Household Humor

Q: Why did the house go to the doctor?
A: Because it had window panes.

Q: What did the house wear to the party?
A: Address.

Q: What did the big chimney say to the little chimney?
A: "You're too young to be smoking."

Q: What did one wall say to the other wall?
A: "Meet me at the corner."

Q: What has four legs but can't walk?
A: A table.

- Did you hear the joke about the roof?
- No.
- Nevermind, it's over your head.

Q: Why did the lady want wheels on her rocking chair?
A: So she could rock and roll.

Q: What did the mommy broom say to the baby broom?
A: "It's time to go to sweep."

Q: Why was the broom late?
A: It over swept.

Q: Why did the computer go to the doctor?
A: Because it had a virus.

Q: Why was the computer so tired when it got home?
A: Because it had a hard drive.

Q: What is a clock's favorite spice?
A: Thyme.

Q: Why did the portrait go to jail?
A: Because someone framed it.

Q: Where do books like to sleep?
A: Under their covers.

Q: What did the blanket say to the bed?
A: "Don't worry, I've got you covered."

Q: What is the last thing you take off before you go to bed?
A: Your feet off the ground.

Q: Why do you go to bed every night?
A: Because the bed won't come to you.

Q: What do you feed a teddy bear?
A: Nothing; it's already stuffed.

Q: How do you get on television?
A: You climb on top of it.

Q: What once was red that now is black?
A: A match.

Q: What has one eye but cannot see?
A: A sewing needle.

Q: How do you make a tissue dance?
A: Put a little boogie in it.

Q: Who stole the soap?
A: The robber ducky.

I was going to look for my missing watch, but I could never find the time.

Q: Why did Tigger have his head in the potty?
A: He was looking for Pooh.

Q: What did the scarf say to the hat?
A: "You go on ahead; I'll hang around here."

Q: Why was the belt arrested?
A: Because it held up some pants.

Q: What's the difference between one yard and two yards?
A: A fence.

Q: What do you call a song sung in an automobile?
A: A car-tune.

Q: What is the most tired part of your car?
A: The exhaust pipe.

Q: Why is a bicycle always exhausted?
A: Because it's two-tired.

Confucius says, "Man who runs behind car gets exhausted."

Q: What kind of car does Mickey's wife drive?
A: A Minnie van.

Earth, Sea and Space

Q: What is the fastest country in the world?
A: Russia.

Q: What is the most slippery country in the world?
A: Greece.

Q: What did Tennessee?
A: The same thing Arkansas.

- Did you like the restaurant on the moon?
- No, it had no atmosphere.

Q: What did Delaware?
A: Her New Jersey.

Q: Where do pencils come from?
A: Pennsylvania.

Q: What would you call the United States if everyone bought a pink car?
A: A pink carnation.

Q: What did one tornado say to the other tornado?
A: "Twist you later!"

Q: What is a tornado's favorite game?
A: Twister.

Q: What do you get when you cross a stream and a brook?
A: Wet feet.

Q: Why was the scarecrow promoted?
A: Because he was outstanding in his field.

Q: What do you call a boomerang that doesn't work?
A: A stick.

Q: What is brown and sticky?
A: A stick.

Q: What has two spines and millions of ribs?
A: A railroad track.

Q: How do trains hear?
A: Through their engine-ears.

Q: What did the water say to the boat?
A: Nothing; it just waved.

Q: What do you get when you throw a million books into the ocean?
A: A title wave.

Q: What do sea monsters eat for lunch?
A: Fish and ships.

Q: Why did the sea monster eat five ships that were carrying potatoes?
A: Because no one can eat just one potato ship.

Q: What lies at the bottom of the sea and shakes?
A: A nervous shipwreck.

Q: What happens when you throw a green stone into the Red Sea?
A: It gets wet.

Q: How do you organize a space party?
A: You planet.

Q: What kind of plates are used in space?
A: Flying saucers.

Q: Why did Mickey Mouse go to outer space?
A: Because he wanted to see Pluto.

Q: What did the astronaut realize when he found bones on the moon?
A: The cow didn't make it.

Q: If athletes get athlete's foot, what do astronauts get?
A: Missile toe.

Q: What do you do when you see a spaceman?
A: Park your car, man.

Q: What did Mars say to Saturn?
A: "Give me a ring sometime."

Q: Why didn't the sun go to college?
A: Because it already had a million degrees.

Athletic Amusement

Q: Why is tennis such a loud sport?
A: Because the players raise a racquet.

Q: At what sport do waiters do really well?
A: Tennis, because they're really good servers.

Q: Why did the man keep doing the backstroke?
A: Because he had just eaten and didn't want to swim on a full stomach.

Q: What is a cheerleader's favorite color?
A: Yeller.

Q: What is a cheerleader's favorite drink?
A: Root beer.

Q: How is a baseball team similar to a pancake?
A: They both need a good batter.

Q: What do basketball players and babies have in common?
A: They both dribble.

Q: What is a ghost's favorite position in soccer?
A: Ghoul keeper.

Q: What is an insect's favorite sport?
A: Cricket.

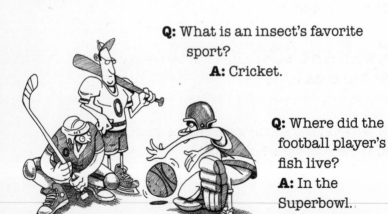

Q: Where did the football player's fish live?
A: In the Superbowl.

Q: Why do some football players never sweat?
A: Because of all their fans.

Q: Why did the football coach go to the bank?
A: He wanted his quarter back.

Q: What do hockey players and magicians have in common?
A: Both do hat tricks.

Q: Why did the hockey player go to jail?
A: Because he shot the puck.

Kid: Doctor, will I be able to play the hockey after the cast comes off?
Doctor: Yes, of course.
Kid: Great! I never could before.

Q: What is the hardest part about skydiving?
A: The ground.

Q: What is harder to catch the faster you run?
A: Your breath.

Q: Why did the golfer wear two pairs of pants?
A: In case he got a hole in one.

Q: What's a golfer's favorite letter?
A: Tee.

Q: Why did Tarzan spend so much time on the golf course?
A: He was perfecting his swing.

Q: Why did the ballerina quit?
A: Because it was tutu hard!

Q: Why was Cinderella not good at football?
A: Because she had a pumpkin as a coach.

Q: Why can't Cinderella play soccer?
A: Because she's always running away from the ball.

Q: Which football player wears the biggest helmet?
A: The one with the biggest head.

 Knock Knock Randoms

Knock knock.
Who's there?
Nobody.
Nobody who?
(Stay silent)

Knock knock.
Who's there?
Tank.
Tank who?
You're welcome.

Knock knock.
Who's there?
Little old lady.
Little old lady who?
I didn't know you could
  yodel!

Knock knock.
Who's there?
Yourself.
Yourself who?
Your cell phone's ringing.
  You should answer it.

Knock knock.
Who's there?
Nobel.
Nobel who?
No bell, that's why
  I knocked!

Knock knock.
Who's there?
Hatch.
Hatch who?
Bless you, but please cover
  your mouth next time.

Knock knock.
Who's there?
Hawaii.
Hawaii who?
I'm fine. How are
  you?

Knock knock.
Who's there?
Queen.
Queen who?
Queen as a whistle.

Knock knock.
Who's there?
Dozen.
Dozen who?
Dozen anyone want
  to let me in?

Knock knock.
Who's there?
Yacht.
Yacht who?
Yacht a know me
  by now.

Brain Twisters

Q: What doesn't get any wetter no matter how much it rains?
A: The ocean.

Q: A guy went out in pouring rain with no umbrella or hat or anything. Not a hair on his head got wet. How come?
A: He was bald. He didn't have a hair on his head.

Q: When is a car not a car?
A: When it turns into a garage.

Q: A woman left her keys and her baby in the car. The car was locked. Why wasn't she worried?
A: The car was a convertible with the top down.

Q: Imagine you are on a deserted island with no method of communication. You have to get off. There are evil things surrounding the island. How do you get off?
A: Stop imagining it.

Q: A man rode into town on his horse on Tuesday. A week later, he left on Friday. How is this possible?
A: His horse's name was Friday.

Q: What runs but never walks?
A: Water.

Q: A dancer's sister died. The woman who died had no sisters. How was this possible?
A: The dancer was a man.

Q: If a cat can jump five feet high, then why can't it jump through a three-foot-high window?
A: The window is closed.

Q: What is the longest word in the English language?
A: Smiles, because between the first and last letter there is a mile.

Q: Janet and Joan were found dead in a room which had an open window. And, there were glass splinters in a puddle of water on the floor. How did they die?
A: A gust of wind blew through the open window, knocking the glass fish bowl to the floor. The bowl broke, and the two fishes, Janet and Joan, died.

Q: As I was going to St. Ives, I saw a man with seven wives. The seven wives had seven sacks; the seven sacks had seven cats; the seven cats had seven rats; rats, cats, sacks, wives—how many were going to St. Ives?
A: One (me).

Q: What is the only thing that you can put into a bucket that will make it lighter?
A: A hole.

Q: What has a mouth but doesn't eat, a bank but no money, a bed but doesn't sleep, and waves but no hands?
A: A river.

Q: What is the difference between a cat and a dog?
A: Dogs think, "Humans are benevolent, they feed me and take care of me, so they must be gods. Cats think, "Humans are benevolent, they feed me and take care of me, so I must be God."

Q: Four cats are in a boat. One jumps out. How many are left?
A: None. They were all copy cats.

Q: A man lives and works in the same building. Every day he takes the elevator from the 10th floor down to the 1st floor where he works. At the end of the day he rides from the 1st floor up to the 7th floor and takes the stairs the rest of the way. Why?
A: He is a little person and can't reach the 10th floor button.

Q: What gets bigger and bigger as you take more away from it?
A: A hole.

Q: How many months have 28 days?
A: All of them.

Q: What kind of button won't unbutton?
A: A bellybutton.

Q: What goes up when the rain comes down?
A: An umbrella.

Q: What gives you the power and strength to walk through walls?
A: A door.

Q: What kind of bow cannot be tied?
A: A rainbow.

Q: What only starts to work after it's been fired?
A: A rocket.

Q: What goes up but never comes down?
A: Your age.

ABOUT THE AUTHOR

James Allan Einstein has been collecting kids jokes of all kinds since...well...since he was a kid! In fact, he still thinks of himself as a great big kid because he still gets a kick out of grossing people out with vomit and bathroom jokes, and he also loves the quintessential knock-knock joke! Invariably, his friends will groan when he says excitedly, "I've got a new one for you!"

ABOUT THE ILLUSTRATORS

Roger Garcia Einstein is a self-taught freelance illustrator who works in acrylics, ink and digital media. His illustrations have been published in humor books, children's books, newspapers and educational material.

When Roger is not at home drawing, he gives cartooning workshops at various elementary schools, camps and local art events. Roger also enjoys participating with colleagues in art shows and painting murals in schools and public places.

Peter Tyler Einstein is a graduate of the Vancouver Film School's Visual Art and Design and Classical animation programs. Though his ultimate passion is in filmmaking, he is also intent on developing his draftsmanship and storytelling, with the aim of using those skills in future filmic misadventures.

Gerry Dotto Einstein was born and raised in Sherwood Park, Alberta, where his obsession with the color red led him to become a graphic designer. Today, he designs using other colors—not just his favored red.

When he's not at his computer desk, you might find him playing baseball, watching hockey or dancing down the street when a good song starts playing on his iPod. Some people refer to him as the "Mustache Man" for the epic mustache he sports on his top lip—and when he drinks chocolate milk, his milk mustache is the king of them all.